BELGIUM TRAMS AND TROLLEY BUSES

JOHN LAW

First published 2022

Amberley Publishing
The Hill, Stroud
Gloucestershire, GL5 4EP

www.amberley-books.com

Copyright © John Law, 2022

The right of John Law to be identified as
the Author of this work has been asserted in
accordance with the Copyrights, Designs and
Patents Act 1988.

ISBN 978 1 3981 0724 3 (print)
ISBN 978 1 3981 0725 0 (ebook)

All rights reserved. No part of this book may be
reprinted or reproduced or utilised in any form
or by any electronic, mechanical or other means,
now known or hereafter invented, including
photocopying and recording, or in any information
storage or retrieval system, without the permission
in writing from the Publishers.

British Library Cataloguing in Publication Data.
A catalogue record for this book is available from
the British Library.

Origination by Amberley Publishing.
Printed in the UK.

Introduction

Belgium is a young country, coming into existence around 1830 after separating from the Netherlands. It was initially French speaking. Without wishing to enter local politics, it is safe to say that the country is divided by language. In Flanders a form of Dutch is used, while the citizens of Wallonia have their own version of French. The country's capital, Brussels, is officially bilingual, though the local dialects have a mixture of words from as many languages as there have been invaders. It should also be mentioned that there is a small German-speaking area in the east of the country, ceded to Belgium in 1919.

Throughout this book, the local name for the locations are used, thus it is Antwerpen, not Antwerp or Anvers. Likewise, Liège rather than Leuk (Flemish) or Lüttich (German). However, not wishing to cause an international incident, the English name for the capital, Brussels, will be used.

My late friend, Tony Martens, though residing in London, was a Belgian citizen and was able to visit his homeland from the 1960s onwards, photographing many of the country's famous tram locations, such as Liège, Mons and Verviers, all of which have now lost their tramways. Sadly Tony passed away in 2019, but I have been able to access his slide collection, providing a marvellous selection from the 1960s and early 1970s.

My first visit to the country was, if my memory serves me well, in 1971, though it was only for one night. That was still long enough to see the four-wheelers in Brussels and sample the few remaining lines of the Brabant Vicinal network. I have since become a regular visitor and, of course, I always have my camera with me. Between Tony and myself, we have been able to put together the selection within these pages, covering approximately sixty years.

The first tramway in Belgium was opened in 1869 using horse traction, with electrification coming from 1894 onwards. As befitting the capital, it soon became the country's largest network and it is today the only one using standard gauge tracks. The city of Brussels now has a metro system, but how this came about is of interest. Like many European cities, many tram routes were diverted underground, but Brussels decided on the 'pre-metro', wherein full-size metro stations were built, but at first only served by trams before later being converted to full metro specifications. The latest news is that the tram network is set to be expanded with an extension reaching Brussels International Airport at Zaventem by 2026.

There were once trolleybuses in Brussels, though this period was relatively short-lived. Commencing in 1939, they ran from Forest in the south, through the city centre to Machelen in the north. Operations ceased in 1964.

Antwerpen is the second largest city in Belgium and has a tram system reflecting that fact. The first tram route, using horse haulage, commenced in 1873, running from Berchem to Meir, the main shopping street in the city centre. Expansion and electrification followed, converting the standard gauge track to the narrower metre gauge. Electric trams began running in 1902, a situation still existing today. In 1991, Antwerpen's public transport was transferred to De Lijn, set up to take over all bus, tram and trolleybus services in Vlaanderen (Flanders). Today, much of the tram lines in the city centre are below ground metro-style, but, at the time of writing, it is still possible to ride through the narrow streets to the Melkmarkt terminal loop.

The was also a short-lived trolleybus system in Antwerpen, running between 1929 to 1964. One of the trolleybuses is preserved in the museum in Berchem.

The third Belgian city to introduce trams was Gent, with horse-drawn cars starting in 1874. Electricity came later, in the form of battery-operated trams, replaced by normal overhead wire current collection from 1904. The pleasant blue colour scheme was, after 1991, replaced by the standard white livery of De Lijn. Unlike those of Antwerpen, Gent's trams are capable of being driven from both ends, as there are no turning circles.

An unusual development in Gent was the introduction of trolleybuses, as late as 1989, when a tram route to Gentbrugge was converted. This too ended up in the De Lijn empire but, being non-standard, it only lasted twenty years and thus Belgium's last trolleybuses ceased operating in 2009.

Liège was the second city in Belgium to embrace railed street transport, with horse-drawn trams starting in 1871 and electrification underway from 1893. On 10 August 1930 tram route 20 (Cathédrale–Cointe) was converted to trolleybus operation. Eventually, Liège was able to boast that it had the largest trolleybus network in Belgium. At one time the unique double-ended trolleybus operated here. It is now preserved in the city. Trolleybus operations ceased in 1971, outliving the city's trams, which stopped running in 1968. However, a new tram system is now under construction.

Charleroi, in French-speaking Hainault Province, began tramway operations in 1881, again with horse-drawn vehicles. Electrification came from 1904 and a sizeable network was soon in place. In 1962, Société des Transports Intercommunaux de Charleroi (STIC) assumed control and continued to operate trams until TEC took over all Wallonian public transport in 1991. This brought the local Vicinal lines, as well as STIC trams, under one management. The current situation is that the trams in the city centre are at the 'pre-metro' stage, while roadside running is still partly in operation on the former Vicinal route to Anderlues.

The small tram system in Verviers, a city in the Province of Liège, was in operation from 1884 to 1969. It consisted of five routes. Like the other city-based operations, it began with horse haulage, with electrification following from 1900.

So far we have seen that tramways developed in Belgium like those of Great Britain, or most other cities in Europe. But Belgium had something that was both different and virtually unique. It had the Vicinal. Les Tramways Vicinaux or De Buurtspoorwegen built up a huge network of metre gauge light railways throughout the country. The route mileage even exceeded that of the national (standard gauge) rail network. Most of the system consisted of roadside tramways, though not exclusively. Of course, economics prevailed and much of the network were closed – by the 1970s very few routes still operated. The remaining lines into central Brussels ceased operations in 1978.

All that remains of the former Vicinal network today is the Kusttram, which runs the entire length of the Belgian coast, plus part of the Charleroi Metro. There are, however, a couple of preservation sites, plus the diesel-operated tourist line at Han-sur-Lesse.

And the future? Well, trams are due to return to Liège and an even bigger development is the construction of a light rail system linking Hasselt (in Limburg Province) with the Dutch city of Maastricht. Whether that happens is in the hands of the politicians, but some new tram tracks have been noted beside Hasselt railway station.

I am grateful to the following for supplying a few photographs: Tim Boric, Richard Huggins, Vitaly Volkov and the Industrial Railway Society.

In the 1960s and early 1970s, four-wheel trams were still common in Brussels. A total of 685 cars were built up until in the 1930s. They were rebuilt over the years to more modern standards. They usually ran with a trailer car in tow; here, in a typical example, car No. 1266 hauls a trailer through the city centre on route 62.

Running as just a single car, No. 1403 is seen on route 74 in the city centre on a wet day, as the *friture* in the side street receives some custom. Together with the mixture of weather-beaten buildings forming the backdrop, this is a typical scene in the capital in the late 1960s.

Back in 1971, Place Rogier in the city centre of Brussels was a hole in the ground, surrounded by tram lines. Seen from one of the hotels, a four-wheel tram and trailer bisect one of the other lines. It will be noted that the curve on the far left of the picture is of metre gauge and was used by the Vicinal services still running at the time.

Here we are beside the austere exterior of Brussels Zuid/Midi railway station, as four-wheel car No. 1442 negotiates the curves on route 55.

Belgium Trams and Trolley Buses

Some of the four-wheel cars were rebuilt in the early 1960s with new coachwork. Numbered in the 9000 series, they were the first Brussels trams to be capable of one-person operation. Here, No. 9055 was captured on film in the city centre.

Similar car No. 9062 lived a bit longer than most of the batch, as it was exported to Scotland and operated at the Summerlee Industrial Museum from 1988 to 2004. Sadly, it suffered terminal vandalism and was scrapped, though parts went to help other museums. It was photographed operating in September 1998.

The first bogie cars to be introduced to the Brussels system came in the form of the 5000 class, ordered in 1935. Twenty-five cars were ordered, one of which, No. 5010, is seen near Zuid/Midi railway station c. 1970. All this batch were withdrawn from normal service by 1976.

Bogie car No. 5001 has fortunately been preserved. At one time it had been fitted with an additional centre entrance, but has since been rebuilt to its original configuration. No. 5001 is now a regular performer on the city tour and is seen at Schaarbeek station on 30 September 2017.

The 7000 series of tramcars for Brussels was built over a twenty-year period from 1951 onwards. Though they were constructed in Belgium, they incorporated bogies, both new and second-hand, built by PCC (Presidents Conference Committee) in the United States. Here, in 1971, we see a rear view of car No. 7138 at Place Rogier. Though single-ended, these cars were capable of being driven from the rear for shunting movements and at 'Y'-shaped termini. The bogies on this particular car came from an older PCC streetcar in Kansas City. Note the dual gauge track on the left, to accompany the Vicinal services.

Brussels car No. 7108 is seen in one of the 'pre-metro' sections, arriving at Kunst-Wet/Arts Loi station in the city centre. Opened in 1969, this facility had lost its trams by 1976, when full-size metro trains took over.

Another of the 7000 series, No. 7153 was photographed leaving the various stops in the gloom below Brussels Zuid/Midi railway station some time around 1970. It appears to have a good load aboard! It can be seen that the tram has both a pantograph and a trolley pole attached to its roof, the latter being in use here.

No. 7166 also emerges from the same place. This was one of a small batch of the 7000 series built in 1970/1.

No. 7063 is seen here as it approaches Brussels Zuid/Midi railway station in the summer of 1983. Trams no longer run at street level past Bar Asturias (seen on the right with the ubiquitous 'Jupiler' sign) on Boulevard Jamar, as they now vanish underground at this point.

Some of the 7000 series trams lasted long enough to receive the yellow and blue colours, as seen on No. 7067, heading for Brussels Zuid/Midi railway station on 1 March 2007. All of this type of tram has since been withdrawn.

The tram series 4000, numbered 4001 to 4043, was introduced in 1963, as three-piece articulated sets. The first in the batch, No. 4001, was photographed outside Zuid/Midi station around 1970. One of these trams, No. 4025, now resides in the Brussels tram museum at Woluwe-Saint-Pierre.

The museum mentioned above is well worth a visit and, as it has connections with the main network, is able to run some of its collection through the city streets on certain occasions. On 1 June 1997 car No. 410 was photographed outside the museum, a former depot. The 1903-built car is in the livery of Les Chemins de Fer Economiques, one of the constituents of what was to become STIB/MIVB, the current operator of public transport in Brussels. (Richard Huggins)

Belgium Trams and Trolley Buses

Brussels trams numbered 7701 to 7827 were built in Belgium during 1971 and the following year. Like earlier cars, they used PCC components. Those with numbers beginning 77XX were new as single-ended cars, but later were rebuilt with cabs at both ends. Typical of the batch, No. 7758 is seen on route 56 in the city centre on 1 March 2007.

Sister set No. 7760 was also photographed on 1 March 2007, again serving route 56. The location is close to Zuid/Midi railway station.

Tram No. 7804 was built as a double-ended set and is seen here in the Brussels suburbs at Stockel. Wearing the latest livery, it was photographed on 16 September 2010.

While the 7700 series trams were originally single-ended, the 7900 type cars had a driving cab at each end. Built in 1977/8, they were effectively two PCC type cars coupled together, with a centre portion and two pantographs. Here we have No. 7911 on Boulevard Jamar in summer 1993.

The 7900 series cars were later to receive the new gold and silver colour scheme, as applied to No. 7942 when photographed at Brussels West station interchange on 16 September 2010.

The Brussels tramway operator, STIB/MIVB, had (at the time of writing) a total of seven depots. Photographed in 1971 is the one on Avenue du Roi/Koningslaan in Saint-Gilles district. Information to hand suggests that it can hold sixty-three trams. Car No. 7021 is passing on route 81.

The latest Brussels trams are in the 3000 and 4000 series, on which construction started in 2005. Built by Bombardier and featuring low-floor technology, a total of 220 were received. No. 3033 is seen at Schaarbeek terminus in the latest livery. It will depart in two minutes on 30 September 2017.

Also at Schaarbeek terminus on 30 September 2017 is low-floor set No. 3029, in a lurid advertising livery that contrasts with the classic architecture of the railway station behind. The tram appears to have been involved in some kind of scrape at some time and the Belgian version of Gaffer Tape has been applied to the front end.

Though there had been horse-drawn trams in Antwerpen since 1873, it was not until Tuesday 2 September 1902 that Compagnie Générale des Tramways d'Anvers (French being the official language then) began operating electric trams. The earliest trams were, of course, four-wheelers with trailers soon being built to accommodate demand. Here is a postcard view of Meir Plaats, the city's main shopping area, with tram 441 and trailer. The motor car was part of a batch, 401 to 471, built between 1904 and 1913. This photograph can therefore be dated as *c.* 1910.

Some of the two-axle trams were destined to have a long life. Here is car No. 6349, originally numbered 349, one of the batch built from 1902 onwards. This is one of those that were rebuilt around 1948 that became known as 'type 351'. They were slightly longer than the earlier ones. The few cars that had such a prolonged period of service survived until 1974, but this photograph is believed to have been taken in the late 1960s. It shows the tram exiting Keyserslei as it passes Centraal station, where the photographer is situated.

Another of the 'type 351' four-wheel trams, No. 6353 is seen on Stationsplein passing the Billard Palace, a mixture of billiard room and hotel that survives to this day.

The batch of trams originally numbered 522 to 551 were delivered in 1930. They turned out to be the last two-axle cars for the Antwerpen system. Most of them were withdrawn in the 1960s, but the last seven pushed on into 1970. Six went from scrap, but No. 4550 was saved for preservation. Here it is in the museum at Schepdaal in 1971, though it now resides in Antwerpen's tram museum.

The first batch of so-called 'PCC' cars for Antwerpen, built in Belgium, were delivered in 1960 and the following year numbered 2000 to 2038. They were painted in the cream livery with brown lining, as displayed by car No. 2009 negotiating Stationsplein by Centraal station.

Here we have another of the same series, No. 2008, this time photographed at the Groenplaats stop in the heart of the city, close to Antwerpen's cathedral.

The 'PCC' cars became the standard for Antwerpen, with 166 being delivered in total – the last examples arriving in 1975. The operator for the period 1960 to 1991 was Maatschappij voor het Intercommunaal Vervoer te Antwerpen (MIVA). In that company's livery is No. 2016, seen close to Centraal station in the summer of 1983.

The Astrid Theatre in Antwerpen lies across the square from Centraal station and is passed by a frequent tram service. Car No. 2086, one of the 1962 batch, speeds by, heading for the city centre on route 24.

Belgium Trams and Trolley Buses

A one-way loop takes trams around Stationsplein, bringing them in front of Antwerpen's Centraal station, which is where we see 'PCC' car No. 2050 sometime aound 1970.

The first section of 'pre-metro' below surface line opened in 1975, running from Keyserslei to Groenplaats, with underground stops at Opera and Meir. 'PCC' car Nos 2133 and 2086 are seen at the Groenplaats station, not long after opening. The subsurface route was, in 1980, to serve Antwerpen Centraal station, confusingly by two stops called Plantin and Diamant. Later extensions saw the tramway pass under the Schelde towards Linkeroever.

A final view of a 'PCC' car in the old MIVA colours, as No. 2068 comes off Meir and joins with the line from Pelikaanstraat to enter Stationsplein.

For a few years, towards the end of MIVA control, Antwerpen's tram received this red-based colour scheme, as seen on 'PCC' car No. 2090, in tandem with a sister as it heads out of the city on Gemeentestraat in summer 1983.

De Lijn took over all public transport in the Flemish speaking provinces in 1991. A white livery was adopted, though the two 'PCC' cars seen here on the Stationsplein loop in Antwerpen during 4 March 2007 are both wearing advertising vinyls. The 1990s saw a refurbishment programme and these cars renumbered in the 7XXX series. No. 7042 waits for passengers on route 12.

'PCC' car No. 7043 was also photographed in advertising colours as it runs down the middle of the street in the suburb of Hoboken, 9 March 2009.

Most trams in the old centre of Antwerpen are now sent below ground, but one line, service 11, still traverses the narrow streets around the Melkmarkt loop. Seen there on 25 June 2009 is 'PCC' car No. 7014, heading for Eksterlaar. Route 11 has since been cut back to Bercham railway station.

It is common for the 'PCC' cars in Antwerpen to run around coupled into pairs, as witnessed by the photographer here on 18 September 2010. Here we see No. 7063 and a friend in the suburban streets of Bercham.

There were 166 'PCC' cars in total delivered for the Antwerpen system and a good number of them are seen inside Hoboken depot ('remise Zwaantjes') on 9 March 2009.

Antwerpen tram route 24 once ran around the Melkmarkt loop, but since 2019 has been diverted to serve the new line to Havenhuis via the Mexicobrug, a lift bridge in the city's docks. This structure used to carry railway tracks. Here we see 'PCC' car No. 7116 on the new section, just after opening on 11 December 2019. (Tim Boric)

The first low-floor trams for De Lijn's Antwerpen system arrived in 1999 and 2000, numbered 7201 to 7231. Nicknamed 'HermeLijn' trams, a derivation of the Dutch word for stoat, they were made up of three motor sections, plus the two longer non-powered pieces. Here we see No. 7214 at the Harmonie stop, bound for Mortsel, on 6 March 2007.

One of the second batch of 'HermeLijn' low-floor sets, No. 7236, delivered in 2004, was photographed at Merksem terminus on 20 September 2010. It will traverse route 3 under the Schelde to Linkeroever and then over the new extension to Zwijndrecht.

Another of the 'HermeLijn' sets, No. 7214, takes a rest on the terminating loop at Mortsel, where there are several convenient hostelries, 18 September 2010.

The route via Mortsel was considerably extended in 2012 and now reaches a park-and-ride facility at Boechout. It is here, on 7 October 2019, that we see one of the latest 'Albatrossen' low-floor sets, No. 7307. More than 40 metres in length, these vehicles have a capacity of 266 passengers and consist of seven sections. There are now also some 'Korte Albatrossen' sets, of just five pieces.

Antwerpen's tram museum is located in an old depot in Berchem, which had become redundant in 1996. Within are trams and buses from various parts of Vlaanderen, with a good representation from Antwerpen itself. One of the exhibits is this four-wheel car, one of the 401 series, converted to a ballast tipper vehicle. It was photographed at home on 18 September 2010.

One of two prototype trams bought for the Antwerpen system, No. 200 was the forerunner of a huge batch of similar two-axle cars. It has pride of place inside the museum, again on 18 September 2010.

Belgium Trams and Trolley Buses

29

The first of the 'PCC' cars for Antwerpen, No. 2000, has been lovingly restored to its red livery and was photographed in the museum on 18 September 2010.

Trolleybuses in Antwerpen ran from 1929 until 30 March 1964. At the height of the system, three routes operated. Fortunately one of the small vehicles, No. 45, has been preserved and is seen inside the museum.

In the 1960s the city of Gent relied on a fleet of rather ancient two- and three-axle trams. The hub of the network was Korenmarkt where six-wheel car Nos 326, 350 and 360 were photographed by Tony Martens.

The beating heart of Gent, around Korenmarkt at Graslei, is a good distance from the city's main railway station, Gent-Sint-Pieters. Fortunately, today's No. 1 tram service will transport you swiftly and frequently between the two. Sometime around the late 1960s, six-wheel car No. 352 has just started out on its journey from Sint-Pieters station on route 10 to Muidebrug via the city centre.

Another of the antiquated three-axle trams, No. 321, was found at Sint-Pieters station, again on route 10. The tram network was reduced somewhat in the 1960s, but a service to Muidebrug still operates today.

The streets of the shopping area of Gent city centre are very narrow and the trams are obliged to use a one-way system to access the Korenmarkt area from the south. Here we see car No. 350 negotiating through the traffic on its way to Sint-Pieters station on service 4.

A fine view of three-axle car No. 317 travelling through the streets of suburban Gentbrugge, heading for Melle, a route that ceased operations in 1973. Wrong way working was the norm here, as that little car takes avoiding action!

Car Nos 330 and 317 are seen negotiating a passing loop on the Brusselsesteenweg in Gentbrugge. The closest tram has just passed under the railway linking Gent-Sint-Pieters station with Dampoort and beyond.

Belgium Trams and Trolley Buses

Now we are a little further towards the north-west along the Brusselsesteenweg and three-axle tram 361 speeds away from the camera. It is passing the unusual barrel-shaped bar De Ton (The Tun in English). Trams still pass this point but use a new formation in the middle of a dual carriageway. It is pleasing to note that De Ton is still open for business and has even had a small beer garden installed in the front.

It was noted earlier that Gent also ran four-wheel trams, though most had vanished by the time either of our photographers visited the city. However, this two-axle car, numbered 173 and converted for departmental use, was found by Tony Martens in the nearby depot yard, no doubt after a visit to De Ton.

Since 1961, MIVG (Maatschappij voor Intercommunaal vervoer te Gent) had operated public transport in Gent. Both buses and trams shared the depot in Gentbrugge and MIVG had adopted a blue and cream colour scheme, though it was not applied to the old three-axle trams. In 1971, the first of the new 'PCC' cars was introduced and one can be seen in this view of the main depot.

The first route to receive the 'PCC' type trams was No. 4, in 1971, and it is around that time that car No. 07 was photographed at Gent-Sint-Pieters station.

'PCC' car No. 52 is seen on the turning loop at Gent-Sint-Pieters station in the summer of 1983. Most of Gent's tram termini, however, had no such facilities and the 'PCC' cars and their successors had driving cabs at both ends.

The Gravensteen, a medieval castle in the heart of Gent city centre, forms the backdrop to this photograph of car No. 45 operating route 1 in the mid-1970s.

The Gent tram undertaking, MIVG, was taken over by De Lijn in 1991 and the standard white livery soon adopted. 'PCC' car No. 42 was lucky enough to receive advertising to break up the monotony. It was photographed in mid-1992 at the Korenmarkt stop, in front of the fine old post office building. Though trams still pass this point, the boarding points here have been moved to other nearby streets.

De Lijn car No. 6209 was one of twenty-two to be refurbished and became known as 'PCC2' types. The differences can clearly be seen in this photograph at Gent-Sint-Pieters station on 29 June 2009.

'PCC2' No. 6217 is loading up at Korenmarkt on route 4 to Moscou on 4 March 2008 as another tram of the same batch is heading for Gent-Sint-Pieters station on a fairly indirect route.

When De Lijn in Gent received its first low-floor 'HermeLijn' trams, they differed from those of Antwerpen in that they could be driven from either end, a situation necessitated by termini such as this one at Moscou. Car No. 6302 was photographed there on 28 June 2009 on service 4 to Korenmarkt, a short working due to engineering work in the city centre.

'HermeLijn' set No. 6341 is seen at the Korenmarkt stop on a sunny 4 March 2008.

Like Antwerpen, De Lijn in Gent has now gained some seven-piece 'Albatrostrams'. No. 6352 was photographed at Evergem Brielken terminus to the north of the city on 12 February 2017. (Wikimedia Commons, Creative Commons)

In September 2004 Gent celebrated the centenary of its electric trams by holding a parade through the city's streets. Here, three-axle tram 328, suitably decorated, leads a pair of four-wheeled trailers.

'PCC' car No. 35, in a dedicated livery, proceeds along the street, as four-wheel tram 216 follows. The latter normally resides in the museum at Antwerpen.

In 1989, Gent tram route 3 was converted to trolleybus operation, with normal diesel-powered buses being deemed unsuitable. Twenty Van Hool AG280T articulated vehicles were obtained by MIVG, one of which, No. 19, is seen in the city centre in mid-1992. It is in its original blue livery, though here operated by De Lijn.

Now in white livery, trolleybus No. 08 is seen running alongside a canal as it heads out of Gent city centre towards Dampoort station and Gentbrugge on 4 March 2008. Operations were to cease in the following year. Some of the trolleybuses were sold for further service in Bulgaria.

Set up in 1962, the Société des Transports Intercommunaux de Charleroi (STIC) operated the trams in the Wallonian city. The network was centred around the city's main railway station, Charleroi Sud, as seen here. A fleet of small four-wheel vehicles was maintained, some of which towed trailers. On the left is car No. 425.

Another Charleroi tram, running alone, No. 404, again at Gare Sud. Because of the livery, the trams were known locally as *les trams verts* ('the green trams').

The two-axle cars could also run in multiple and two are seen here coupled together at Charleroi Sud station. Car No. 409 is closest to the camera.

In addition to the rather angular trailer cars seen earlier, STIC employed some non-powered four-wheel cars, some of which are seen here at the main depot.

Belgium Trams and Trolley Buses

In 1991, the STIC organisation was combined with the Vicinal network (and other operators) to form TEC (Transport en Commun), which was to operate all public transport in French-speaking Wallonia. The tramway was gradually converted into a metro and was partly sent underground in the city centre. At Beaux-Arts station, 1920-built tram 310 and a trailer were exhibited, as seen on 28 February 2008.

TEC's current trams were built in the early 1980s by Belgian company La Brugeoise et Nivelles. They are double-ended articulated vehicles, as shown here, with No. 7416 arriving at Charleroi Gare Sud from the elevated section on 28 February 2008.

Another photograph taken on 28 February 2008, showing tram No. 7442 departing from Gare Sud on a short working to Beaux-Arts.

Though most of the Charleroi TEC metro network is on reserved track or on dedicated rights-of-way, the line to Anderlues, once part of the Vicinal network, in some places is still a roadside tramway. On 28 February 2008, the weather has taken a turn for the worse as No. 7413 waits in the road at Anderlues terminus.

The Société Anonyme des Railways Economiques de Liège-Seraing et Extensions (RELSE), as the name suggests, operated a standard gauge tram network in the Wallonian city of Liège. In 1964, it combined with the city tramway to form la Société des Transports Intercommunaux de Liège (STIL). Large bogie cars were in operation, such as this example, No. 307, photographed outside Liège Guillemans station, the principal SNCB railhead for the city.

STIL operated out towards the south-west of the city of Liège. Seen in the city centre is car No. 312, on a service to Seraing, photographed on 29 May 1966. This type of vehicle, with 135 seats, was delivered in 1933.

Sometime around 1966, bogie car No. 306 has reached the terminal loop at Seraing. At one time, there was interchange here with the trolleybus route to Chatqueue, operated by the unique double-ended vehicles.

On the opposite bank of the River Meuse from Liège, at Pont-de-Seraing, we have a fine view of the city and its industry, as STIL tram No. 320 negotiates the pointwork.

In addition to the normal service using the large bogie cars, STIL ran a shuttle service between Pont-de-Seraing and Seraing itself, using four-wheel cars such as No. 55, seen at the former.

Four-wheel car No. 53 was photographed at Seraing terminus sometime around 1966.

On a showery day we see the STIL tram terminus in central Liège, at Place de la République Française. Car No. 304 waits for departure on service 3 to Flémalle.

The city centre terminus was later repositioned to Place General Leman, near Guillemans station, where we see bogie car No. 313 ready to leave.

This photograph was taken in November 1967 and is recorded as that final day celebrations. The trams of Liège did not cease operations until the following year, so it is presumed that this commemorates the closure of the city centre section. Heritage four-wheel car No. 51 hauls a trailer, both well laden with passengers.

Liège also had a trolleybus system and the most unique vehicles in the fleet were the bidirectional ones, which could be driven from either end. Fortunately, one is preserved in the city's transport museum and was photographed there by Vitaly Volkov. (Vitaly Volkov, Creative Commons)

A more conventional trolleybus, of type VB, is seen in the city of Liège. No. 532 was photographed at Place Saint-Lambert. Trams of both the city and the Vicinal system once served this location and the unused dual gauge trackwork is still visible. There is also a fine 'normal control' motorbus behind.

One of the smaller trolleybuses, No. 515, in service in Liège city centre. Trolleybus operation is the city ceased in 1971.

Verviers is the second largest city in the Province of Liège, not far from the border with Germany. It is a pleasant place that once boasted a small tram network. In a central square, one of the older four-wheel cars, No. 37, passes through. It had been built as long ago as 1928. All these photos in Verviers were taken on 13 April 1968.

The later trams for Verviers had five bay bodies, as seen here with No. 95 rounding a curve in the city centre.

Another of the earlier cars, No. 38, seen in traffic in the city. Like most of the fleet, it carries destination boards rather than roller blinds.

Verviers tram 78 was a modernised car, originally built in 1937. Scrutiny will reveal the differences, but the obvious ones are the side window layout and the provision of destination boxes. Having operated solely four-wheel trams, operations ceased in 1969.

We now take a look at the countrywide Vicinal tram network of metre gauge lines. Originally these were steam operated and carried both passengers and freight. An amazing survivor was that of part of the former Liège via Barchon to Fouron le Comte route, which opened in 1908. The section between the colliery at Trembleur to the SNCB station at Warsage was retained to haul standard gauge wagons on transporters. Steam tram locomotive No. 1075, built by Grand Hornu in 1920, is seen with a small load at Warsage in August 1964. No. 1075 went on into preservation. (Harry Townley, reproduced with the permission of the Industrial Railway Society)

Another steam tram locomotive to survive was 'Type 18' No. 1000, built in 1915 and preserved in fine fettle at the Vlaams Tram en Autobus Museum in Antwerpen, where it was photographed in September 2010.

The Vicinal museum at Schepdaal is home to No. 1066, another of the 'Type 18' steam tram locomotive, one of 126 that were built between 1910 and 1920.

A scene that was typical of the time, showing how the Vicinal was an integral part of the fabric of Belgium. The unelectrified roadside tramway is clearly visible in this pre-First World War view of Lanaken (the current spelling) in Limburg province. The line operated between Maaseik and Lanaken, continuing over the border to Maastricht in the Netherlands. Closure of this section came in 1943.

For the rural Vicinal lines, modernisation came in the form of diesel-powered 'autorails'. These were effectively railbuses, though this one, numbered ART40, was used purely as a locomotive (*tractor*). It was preserved at the museum at Schepdaal and photographed around 1971. On busier routes, these were used to haul passenger trailers and also handled much of the freight traffic over the metre gauge lines.

ART40 now resides in the museum at Antwerpen, where it was photographed in 2010.

It is still possible to travel behind one of the 'autorails' at Han-sur-Lesse in Namur Province. In 1906, a branch of the Vicinal line between Rochefort and Willen opened from Han-sur-Lesse to the Grottes de Han. Even in those days the potential for tourist transport to the cave complex was realised. The service continues to this day. 'Autorail' 159, built by Forges Usines & Fonderies Haine-St-Pierre in 1934, is ready to haul three well-laden trailers to the caves on 28 May 1967. The train will return empty, while its passengers take a subterranean walk back to the village.

By 1997, when this photograph was taken at Han-sur-Lesse, 'autorail' ART90 was being held back in case of a sudden rush or failure. This is the oldest one in service, entering service in 1933, though built on an earlier chassis.

A preserved line operation using 'autorails' is the Tramway Touristique de l'Aisne, taking tourists over the former Vicinal line between Pont d'Érezée and Dochamps. This runs through wooded countryside, unlike most of the Vicinal's roadside lines. AR133 was photographed ready to leave the main boarding point in 1997.

AR133 is seen again, on the return journey, making a stop to allow its passengers to tour the depot/museum at Blier. The line was once part of the Comblain-la-Tour: Manhay–Melreux route, which ceased normal operations in 1959.

Here is one of the last 'autorails' to be built, ART300, constructed in 1947 for use between Ath and Tournai. It was withdrawn in 1960 and went into preservation, as seen here at Schepdaal. The prefix 'ART' stood for 'Autorail Tractor'.

The standard Vicinal bogie trams were actually older cars, but fully rebodied during the 1950s, becoming known as the 'S' types. Here we have No. 10038 with a pair of trailers in central Brussels, on route G to Grimbergen. Some of this type of tram lasted until the 1980s.

In 'as built' condition, car No. 10363 was found in Brussels still in service in the 1960s. It had been built at Braine le Compte in 1949.

'S' type car No. 10483 is seen in central Brussels, alongside 'PCC' standard gauge city tram No. 7034, both on a newly laid track layout near Nord station. The Vicinal car will soon depart for Wemmel.

It is 9 April 1966 and here is 'S' type car No. 10481 in central Brussels. It is forming a departure for Wemmel, a route that was to have twelve more years of life, closing in 1978.

Another 'S' type tram, No. 10474, on the terminal loop in central Brussels, negotiates Rue Georges Matheus/Matheusstraat.

No. 10472 has now reached its suburban terminus at Wemmel. The Vicinal certainly had some impressive buildings at its principal stations, as can be seen in this photograph.

Just beyond Wemmel station was the depot, and No. 10472 has been driven into the yard for a spot of minor attention. No doubt it will soon return to central Brussels.

Another view of the depot at Wemmel, mainly featuring 'S' type car No. 10481.

Another 'S' type car with 1950s bodywork, No. 10439 has just emerged from the Heysel Tunnel on route S to Strombeek. After closure of the narrow gauge Vicinal line, the structure was taken over by the city tram/pre-metro network.

Like the lines to Wemmel and Grimbergen, the S route to Strombeek closed in 1978. On the terminal loop at Strombeek is car No. S9762, another product of type 'S' from the Kuregem works, built in 1956.

The car sheds at Grimbergen were impressive. Ten tracks were more than adequate to handle the number of trams required for the service. Some former freight vehicles, retained for infrastructure work, share the depot with more 'S' type cars.

'S' type car No. 10460 sits in the sun outside the station building at Grimbergen. This town in Vlaams-Brabant is well know for its 'Abbey' beer, though it's no longer brewed by the monks and is outsourced to other Belgian breweries.

Another 'S' type, No. 10470, at Grimbergen terminus in 1971, against a backdrop of the magnificent station building.

Perhaps even more impressive than the Vicinal station building at Grimbergen is this fine example at the small Kempenland town of Brecht, to the north of Antwerpen. It now serves as a fine dining establishment called De Statie. It appears that the line here closed as early as 1940, but public transport has improved recently with the opening of the new Noorderkempen railway station on the high-speed line into the Netherlands. Photograph taken on 16 October 2012.

Another former Vicinal station put to good use is in Ranst, in Antwerpen Province. Now named De Tramstatie, it was on the route from Antwerpen to Lier that was closed to passengers in the 1950s. Seen on 17 September 2010, when it had a good range of beers and jenevers.

The Vicinal tram service from Brussels to the town of Ninove in the province of Oost-Vlaanderen (East Flanders) finally ceased operations in June 1968. Therefore this photograph of No. 10454, another 1950s-built 'S' type, was taken just prior to that. The location is Schepdaal, now the home of the Vicinal museum. Tram services through Schepdaal finally ceased in 1970.

Vicinal services in Mons, the provincial capital of Hainaut Province, soldiered on until 1973. Car No. 41010, another 'S' type built in 1956, is seen at Mons railway station on 28 August 1966.

Belgium Trams and Trolley Buses

We now take a look at the Vicinal system in and around Charleroi. The cultural heart of the city is Eden, which was a great place to photograph trams. On 28 August 1966, car Nos 9652 and 10278 are on routes 41 to Trezegnies and 92 to Thuin respectively.

Charleroi's Gare Sud is the main railway station serving the city, and the main building forms the backdrop of this view of 'S' type car No. 10184.

Tony Martens visited Charleroi on 29 May 1966 and this was the sight that greeted him as he exited Gare Sud. 'S' type car Nos S10175 and S9787 are nearest the camera.

On the same occasion, presumably later in the day, 'S' type Nos 9750 and 10224 are facing the camera at Charleroi Gare Sud.

The Vicinal's main depot in Charleroi was an impressive affair, shared with the company's buses. A fine selection of private cars of the period are visible in this photograph, probably in the early 1970s.

Waiting to enter service at Charleroi depot is car No. S10230.

In the latter days of the Vicinal system based on Charleroi, an important place was Anderlues Junction, where No. S9063 was photographed awaiting connections.

Yet another 'S' class car, No. 10492, seen in the sun at Anderlues terminus.

Inside the depot at La Louviêre is works car No. 21001, built new for such duties in 1954.

Also in La Louviêre depot is works car No. 9896, originally constructed in 1931. It is still bearing the words 'Service des Voies Quaregnon', a reminder of previous operations.

Car No. 10390, one of six built in 1950 for the Braine-le-Compte system, was later transferred to Charleroi's operations. It is seen, slightly battered, at La Louvière depot on 28 August 1966.

To help commemorate the centenary of its electric trams in September 2004, the city of Gent held a parade of preserved vehicles, including Vicinal car No. 9750, complete with trailer.

Four-wheel Vicinal tram No. 9727 was built at Braine-le-Compte in 1930 for operations in the Brussels and Waterloo area. Fortunately, it achieved preservation and was photographed in the early 1970s at Schepdaal Museum.

Also built in 1930, this bogie car, No. 9733, is also seen at Schepdaal in the 1970s.

The museum in Antwerpen houses a number of preserved Vicinal trams, one of which, No. 9785, was photographed here on 18 September 2010. It is a rebody of an earlier 1930-built underframe.

Car No. 10298 was one of only five bogie tramcars purely dedicated to freight traffic. The destination reads, 'Goederendienst', meaning 'goods service'. Introduced in 1943, it too is seen on 18 September 2010 in the Antwerpen museum.

Now we come to the Kusttram, which runs virtually the entire length of the Belgian coast. It is 67 kilometres (42 miles) in length, from Knokke-Heist in the north to De Panne in the south. Approximately in the middle is the seaside town of Oostende, which is where we see car No. 9729. This vehicle had been built at Familleureux in 1930. It appears to be on a short working to De Haan.

It was the norm on the Kusttram services for motor coaches to tow trailers, and spares were kept on hand at Oostende to cope with any sudden rush. Like the 'S' motor cars, the trailers were rebuilt on earlier chassis, to achieve the current standard of the 1950s and 1960s. Here, No. 19686 is standing at Oostende, just in case.

Three four-wheeled cars were built in 1932 for the purpose of carrying luggage along the coastal tramway. On 29 August 1966, No. 10019 was photographed at Oostende.

On a different occasion, sister car No. 10021 is basking in the sun at Oostende. Similar car No. 10020 now resides in the museum at Schepdaal.

Belgium Trams and Trolley Buses

'S' type car No. 9746 has been transferred from the Antwerpen area for assistance in summer operations of the Kusttram and is seen in Oostende displaying 'Dienst' (Service) as a destination.

Because the Kusttram route was equipped with turning loops at termini and strategic locations, the motored cars were single-ended and designated 'SO' types. This enabled trailers to be attached and detached as required. Here we see car No. 9242 (a rebody of a 1908/9 vehicle) with a pair of trailers on the loop at Oostende. Various motor cars and trailers occupy the sidings.

Standing room only! Three well filled trailers are behind a 'SO' motor, awaiting a high summer departure from Oostende.

Car No. 10041, new in 1932, has charge of a pair of trailers in Oostende town centre. This tram has since been preserved.

Another 1932-built 'SO' car, No. 10043, leaves the main Oostende facility with two trailers bound for De Panne.

'SO' car No. 9941 sits in the sun at Oostende forming an extra service in the early 1970s.

With doors only on the nearside, 'SO' tramcar No. 9819 is in the sidings at Oostende with a single trailer, ready to form an extra service. Behind is one of two moveable bridges carrying road and tramway over an important canal. When one was open to waterborne traffic, the other was able to maintain an uninterrupted Kusttram service.

With the NMBS/SNCB Oostende railway station building behind, ex-Antwerpen area 'S' type car No. 9647 forms another 'Extra Dienst'. Though the Vicinal's cream livery excluded advertising, some external boards were carried – one here proclaims the delights of a furniture shop. The other board shows some of the stops served.

Oostende was blessed with a decent-sized building housing the ticket office, staff accommodation, etc. It also served as a terminal for the red-liveried Vicinal buses.

Another 1932-built 'SO' car, No. 10050, rests for a few moments at Oostende, prior to heading north to Knokke-Heist.

Renewal of the 'SO' type cars began in 1980, with the introduction of the first of the six-axle cars. The prototype, No. 6000, was followed in 1982 by forty-nine others for the Kusttram operation. Here we see No. 6008 on a northbound service at Oostende on 8 September 1983.

It is now a wet 8 September 1983 as one of the new Kusttram cars, No. 6034, is seen in Oostende, heading for De Panne.

Tram 6015 was photographed in the sidings at Oostende, before the rain on 8 September 1984. The destination blind reads 'Stelplaats', meaning 'Depot', while a notice by the entrance indicates that it a one-man-operated service ('Eenmansbediening').

In September 1983, the sidings at Oostende are pretty full, as it is early morning. Car No. 6036 is closest to the camera.

Another photograph taken in the summer of 1983, with No. 6025 forming a Knokke-Heist service outside the railway station at Blankenberge, one of many popular resort towns along the Kusttram route.

Since 1993, the Kusttram cars have been extended, gaining a total of eight axles and a low-floor middle section. On 10 March 2009 we see Nos 6014 and 6041 in the rebuilt Oostende station, which was to be demolished.

The new addition to one of the Kusttram cars is seen to good advantage in this view of No. 6030, in advertising livery – out of service ('Geen Dienst') at Oostende on 10 March 2009.

Another photograph taken on 10 March 2009, though the sun is now shining. Car No. 6038 is on a driver training run, speeding along the reserved track near Bredane-aan-Zee, north of Oostende.

In its original formation, car No. 6039 had carried advertising livery, but in this photograph, dated 27 June 2009, it has gained its low-floor portion and standard white De Lijn paintwork. It is sitting on the terminal loop at Knokke-Heist.

Not all of the Kusttram route is segregated from road traffic. In the centre of Middelkerke, to the south of Oostende, car No. 6002 comes through the shopping area on 26 June 2009, heading for De Panne.

The distinctive terminus at the southern end of the line, at De Panne, providing easy transfer to the adjacent NMBS/SNCB railway station. Car No. 6027 will return to Oostende.

On 30 June 2009, Kusttram set No. 6002 departs De Panne for the entire journey through to Knokke-Heist.

Another view of Middelkerke, as car No. 6008 passes through the streets on 26 June 2009, heading south.

We are on the edge of the town of Knokke-Heist, as can be seen, as No. 6006 gets into its long journey to the southern terminus on 27 June 2009.

Car No. 6021 is seen in the coastal town of Sint-Idesbald, not far from its terminus on 26 June 2009.

No. 6014 is on a reserved track section in Knokke-Heist, calling at one of the intermediate stops as it makes its way south on a journey that will take over two hours to complete. Photograph taken on 27 June 2009.

The Kusttram serves the resort of De Haan-aan-Zee (Coq-sur-Mer in French), and the station building there is an amazing survivor of the early days of the line. (Vitaly Volkov, Creative Commons)

In the earlier years of the twenty-first century, several low-floor 'HermeLijn' cars were transferred to the Kusttram operation from other De Lijn networks. Here we seen No. 6332 in Middelkerke on 26 June 2009.

Also in Middelkerke on 26 June 2009 is 'HermeLijn' car No. 7246, imported from use in Antwerpen.

Another view of No. 6332 on a short working, on the reversing loop at Lombardsijde-Westende Bad on 26 June 2009.

Like most tram systems worldwide, the Vicinal had some rolling stock that was not used in revenue-earning service. This four-wheel wagon was used purely within the depot and its yard at Strombeek and was probably hand-propelled.

To maintain rail profiles, this mobile grinding machine was employed and was photographed at Schepdaal Museum, c. 1971.

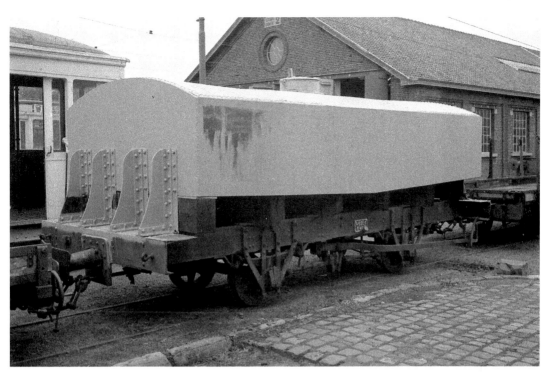

Another exhibit at Schepdaal, this wagon underframe has been adopted to carry a tank, possibly meant to contain diesel fuel for the autorails.

A purpose-built tank car, obviously designed for flammable liquids – hence the 'Defense de Fumer' lettering. La Louvière depot, 28 August 1966.

The Vicinal network once conveyed a significant amount of freight, and vans such as this four-wheel version were commonplace. Fitted with a platform for the brake-man, it is seen in internal use at Het Rad depot near Brussels.

Also at Het Rad is this two-axle open wagon once used for freight on the Brabant system.

More Vicinal freight rolling stock, abandoned in the sidings at Heysel in Brussels.

Road vehicles were also used by the Vicinal for tramway maintenance, etc. This powerful looking three-axle beast would have been used for replacing the traction poles holding up the overhead catenary. It is numbered 36406 and was photographed at Grimbergen depot.

Numbered AT.553 in the Vicinal fleet, this articulated road vehicle, fitted with a rear steering position, would have been used to transfer trams between the various systems. It is seen at La Roue depot, Brussels.

Seen when almost brand new, this Mercedes tower wagon would have been used for overhead line maintenance in the Charleroi area. It was photographed at Anderlues depot, in the company of some smaller departmental road vehicles.